# SUCCEED
## INSIDE THE BOX,
### *GUARANTEED*

RICK GRANDINETTI

## DEDICATION

To my lovely daughters,
Rachel and Geena.

# CONTENTS

# INTRODUCTION

Use your imagination for a moment. Imagine how different your life would be if you improved something in it by 1% every day. 1% does not seem like much of anything does it? I'm here to tell you that it is. For instance, have you ever seen a penny lying on the asphalt and passed it by without picking it up? More than likely you have. Just think, if you picked up an abandoned penny everyday for a hundred days you would be one dollar richer. You would have made a monetary profit just by picking up pennies. 1%! If you changed your life by 1% each day for a year then you would be one-hundred percent better.

Now it is time to hear the flip side of things. If it is good now, it will get worse. If it is bad now, it is going to get horrible. Even so, it doesn't have to be this way. You might be reading this book because you have lost your way, or maybe you are reading this book because you are the company's dinosaur with the pea-sized brain. Overall, it does not matter what your reason is because you are the one on the plane that is passing out the parachutes. We all find ourselves in that position, sooner or later. People lose their passion, companies forget what brought them to the mountaintop, and even powerful nations forget what made them great. However, I have some good news. There is plenty of hope to go around. If you are reading this book, you have come to the right place.

At the beginning of every day, it all comes down to vision. At the end of every day, it is simply whether you had the courage to execute that vision, or not. And most people do not have the courage. Why? Because after all is said and done, more is said than done. Talk is cheap because supply greatly exceeds demand.

Here is your first assignment. Try to change some part of your routine by 1%. Be a person of action. Adopt the following philosophy: ready, fire, aim (That is not a typo). Most people are ready…aim… aim… aim…but they never actually pull the trigger. They do not have the courage. Is it any wonder why they are not successful?

Ignorance on fire is better than knowledge on ice. When people lose their passion, they lose their focus. Want to get rich? Start paying attention to the small things that most people neglect. It is the little things that make a big difference. What little things could you do right now that would make it easier for your customer to do business with you? When individuals lose their way they lose their passion. Passion persuades; it fuels belief and it rarely fails. Remember, it is not the height of your logic that persuades people, it is the depth of your conviction.

There are numerous ways to create success, but just having a great idea does not stop the world on its axis. Great ideas are as common as socks at Wal-Mart. Compare that to people who put ideas into action. Those people are priceless. Be a person of action. Did you know that most ideas are never acted upon? Most techniques or strategies that are taught as information never get applied. Without reinforcement or follow-up, a significant portion of presented information will be forgotten after thirty days. Real change in your behavior only occurs after you have practiced something for twenty-one to thirty-one days.

Knowledge is not power. Never has been. Never will be. Why? Because the business world is loaded with educated idiots. Knowledge is only power when you take action. Your mind is like a parachute. It only works when it is open. Desire to be exceptional; do not look for the exception. These principles are universal common sense, not rocket science. Six years ago, I presented these principles to NASA (the National Aeronautics and Space Administration). Midway through my class, I said, "It doesn't take a rocket scientist to figure these things out." A guy in the back of the room raised his hand and asked, "Rick, do you know what we do for a living?" I said, "No." He said, "We are rocket scientists." He ended his comments, with something that I will never forget. He said, "Rocket science is easy once you understand it. It is like life. It is making common sense a common practice."

Increase your action by 1%. Pull the trigger.

Sooner or later, the bullet's going to hit something, you will never change your life until you change something you do daily by 1%.

# KEYS TO SUCCESS

# GIVE 1% EXTRA EVERYDAY

If you do not change yourself, who will? Are you even willing to change?

If you are not in charge of your own life, then who is?

Improve by 1% every day, and you will never worry about not having enough business or riches in your personal life

On the tombstone of a bishop who lived around 1100 A.D. are the following words: "When I was young and free and my imagination had no limits, I dreamed of changing the world. As I grew older and wiser, I discovered the world would not change, so I shortened my sights somewhat, and decided to change only my country. But my country seemed immovable. As I grew into my twilight years, in one desperate attempt, I settled for trying to change only my family—those closest to me. But alas, my family would have none of it. And now, as I lay on my deathbed, I suddenly realize: if I had only changed myself first, then by example I might have changed my family. With their inspiration and encouragement, I would have then been able to better my country. And who knows? I may have even changed the world."

Be the change you want to see.

If you do not want to change? Welcome to extinction.

If you want to win? Surrender.

That is right. I said "surrender." Winners are people who surrender. Look up the word "surrender" in the dictionary. It basically means joining the winning side.

The world has had many great leaders. But great leaders are only great when they're kneeling.

There is a three letter word called, "Ego". This little word often keeps us from surrendering and being great leaders. Ego causes eighty percent of all problems and prevents ninety-five percent of all solutions. Take that eighty percent off your back. It will make your climb to the mountain top much easier. And when you reach the top of the mountain, it will make breathing a lot easier. Do you really want to wheeze and groan all the way to the top?

Once you achieve your goals, and you are standing at the highest peak in your life, you will find that the air up there is thinner and cleaner. The sun is warmer. The view is magnificent. When you reach the top of the mountain, you will want to spend all your time basking in your accomplishment. Taking time to enjoy everything you worked so hard to achieve. Smelling the pure atmosphere of success.

Do not ruin the journey and the destination by hauling around three-hundred pounds of excess ego. You have carried that load on your back long enough. You have got a mountain to climb now. Just leave your load at the foot of the mountain and get moving.

Surrender, and do just 1% different. Start winning.

Do you actually enjoy interaction with other people? I do.

I like that most of all. Henry David Thoreau said, "The mass of men lead lives of quiet desperation."

Let me add a caveat to that quotation. At night, when most men go to bed, their demons show up. Regrets make them wonder why they are not happy.

---

### Succeeding Inside the Box is Easy...
*Let go of your excess ego and surrender to the winning side.*

# GIVE THE GIFT OF CONSISTENCY

Be consistent.

If you want to be successful at anything—your business, your relationship, your family—you must be consistent.

Many people define consistency as simply exceeding customer expectations. Wrong. Do not start by exceeding your customer's expectations. First, be consistent. If your company cannot even get the old things right, do you really believe that the solution is trying something new? Being consistent is much more important.

Why is consistency so important? Because all products look alike.

Twenty years ago, products had a definite identity, however not in today's market. To the buyer, your product—your airline, your bank, your grocery store, your car dealership—looks just like all the other ones. We live in a sixty-mile-per-hour world. Most of your customers do not have time to discriminate. From coffee to coffins, all products look alike. When people in my seminars hear this concept for the first time, they think, "You do not understand. My company's widgets are different. Our edge over the competition is that we've got glow-in-the-dark colors." Or, "We call ours 'Venti' instead of 'large.' That makes us unique to the customers."

However, to the customers, all products like yours look alike. Let me prove it with one quick example.

I can get on an airplane, and they all look alike to me. It does not matter which airline carrier I use. They all look alike on the inside. The only difference is how that company treats its customers. A smart man once told me, "Fall in love with your customers, not your product. If you do, you will always be successful." Companies that have a great product will not last. Yes. You heard me correctly.

Who will last? "Those who service the best." They will profit the most. Bottom-line? In striving to be successful—in any endeavor—be consistent.

## *Succeeding Inside the Box is Easy...*

*Consistently give the best service.*

# COMMON COURTESIES

Common courtesies are not so common anymore. For instance, what happened to please and thank you or standing up when people introduce themselves to you. The business world is the worst offender of all. I cannot remember the last time someone said, "Thank you for your business." Since people and companies will not make the effort to do these simple things, automation is the order of the day.

One grocery store in my neighborhood is totally self service. It is almost as if the grocery store is saying, "We know we suck at customer service, so just do it yourself". Above the computer is a paper sign that reads, "Thank you." I imagine myself answering back, "You are welcome."

Then, I imagine the computer ending the conversation by saying, "Yes. You are welcome, too. Welcome to take your business elsewhere." And I do.

---

*Succeeding Inside the Box is Easy...*
*All doors open to courtesy.*

## CHANGE FOR A LIFETIME

I have found that overnight success generally takes about fifteen years.

Successful people always focus more on success than failure, yet, ironically, these people have more failures than anybody else. Most people are not surprised by failure. They expect it.

Is it any wonder that eighty-eight percent of our thoughts are negative? Succeeding inside the box is easy. We just stopped doing it.

Individuals and companies cannot stand still. They must constantly be in forward motion. Why? Because even if you are on the right track, and you are standing still, you will get run over.

Let me give you an example. Remember the old expression, "Good enough for government work?" Nowadays, people laugh at government quality. For example: three-thousand dollar hammers, extremely substandard products and shoddy results. Do you realize where the phrase "Good enough for government work," came from? During World War II, that phrase meant "the best in the world!" Back then, women worked in the factories, making all the weapons, the tanks, the guns, and the bullets for their men who were overseas. These women created products that were "the best in the world." Making the best, back then, was literally a matter of life and death. However, somewhere along the line, things changed, people got complacent, and good enough for government work became a joke. Instead of continually improving everything by 1% in government work, employees, managers and leaders stood still and they did get run over.

It is a matter of life and death for your company.

Is your company going to be the next catastrophe, like the U.S. Post Office, or the airlines, or the retail chains? It does not have to be that way. Especially if you resolve to start changing the way you do things.

---

### Succeeding Inside the Box is Easy...

*Improve everything you touch by 1%.*

## GIVE NEGATIVE PEOPLE THE BOOT

Do you know what the funniest thing is about negative people? Most of them do not know they are negative.

Are you one? Sometimes for the greater good someone has to let them know. The result?

If a negative person refuses to change, my advice is to run for the hills. Even if they are family members. Life is too short. Do not waste your time hanging out with negative people. They will suck the life out of you.

Be kind and patient toward other people. In some way, everyone is fighting an internal fight. Make them feel good. Even in a little way.

People might forget what you say, they might forget what you do, however, they will never forget how you make them feel.

---

### *Succeeding Inside the Box is Easy...*
Be remembered for making someone else feel good.

# GUIDING PRINCIPLES

# GIVE EXCELLENT SERVICE

Airlines. Why is it so easy for them to fail?

Once, I was in the Detroit airport terminal. I approached the ticket counter. The agents working behind the counter looked like human beings. In reality, they were vertical coffins. Why? Because they never smiled, and they did not want to be there. The agents hated the customers, and the customers returned the favor. Not a good scene.

I walked up to the counter. The female agent working there never even acknowledged my presence. She was too busy clicking away on her computer. She turned to the agent on her left and said, "I have a year and six months left on this job."

"What does that mean?" I asked. "That is when I retire. I cannot wait to get out of here!" She replied. "Sounds like you are in prison," I said. "Actually," she said, "Yes, I am." Talk about a morale problem.

Can you imagine working alongside that agent? What a horrible existence she had. To her, I was not a customer; I was an intrusion on her work. She was in workplace prison. I was an external customer. She was an internal customer. Simply put, an internal customer is nothing more than an employee. And ninety-eight percent of companies die from the inside out, killed off by internal customers. Employees are not your most valuable asset, the right employees are.

Remember, all products look alike, and those who service the best profit the most. So guess what a company's biggest asset is? It is internal customers. They represent fifty percent of the company income or, fifty percent of the income loss. One of the keys to success is hiring—and keeping—the right internal customers. Some employees are poison. They will sabotage all the good efforts a company can make. To make matters worse, most of the time, these poison employees are not even aware that they are poison. Are you a poison employee at your company? Take good care of your internal customers.

They will take even better care of your external customers.

On another occasion, I was standing in line at the airport terminal, poised behind the yellow line on the floor. That infamous yellow line. The rule is this: you stand behind that yellow line until someone says, "next". Then, you may come forward. Remember, little things make all the difference. Instead of "next" why didn't the agents say, "next passenger in line, please'?" Anyway, I was staring down at the yellow line on the floor.

Meanwhile, not five feet away from me, behind the counter, is an airline agent. She looks very preoccupied and busy with everything except helping the customers.

She might have said, "Excuse me for a moment, sir. I will be right with you." No. At this point, I was not a customer. I was the enemy. Guess what I decided to do?

I crossed the yellow line. I sort of crept up on her and I almost made it to the counter.

Suddenly, the agent's face popped up. She snarled, "I do not remember asking you to cross the yellow line. Get back!"

This is a true story. When companies cease to be in business, they blame the economy, the competition, the high price of oil, or anything else they can think of to avoid dealing with the truth.

Think about these two airline stories. External customers. Internal customers. Having read these two stories, would you find it hard to believe that both of these airlines are now bankrupt? Not me. For all the good things they did, and might have done, these two companies are now bankrupt because of poison employees. These two companies did not get it. Do you?

---

### Succeeding Inside the Box is Easy...
*Remember, those who service the best profit the most. Take good care of your internal customers. They represent fifty percent of the company income or, fifty percent of the income loss.*

# YOUR PATRIOTISM (I AM FLAG)

This is a story about my good friend, Major General. One afternoon, the General and I were golfing at an army base.

Suddenly, it was 5:00 p.m. Do you know what happens on an army base at 5:00 p.m.? The flag comes down. I wasn't familiar with this military custom. I was preparing to hit a long drive and impress the General. Suddenly, I got a weird vibe. When I looked up, I noticed that everyone in sight was facing the nearest flag. Some people were saluting it, some had their hand on their heart. I was stunned by such honor and respect.

At the time, I remember thinking how privileged I was to live in America. Quickly, I put down my driver. I placed my hand over my heart and watched the flag come down.

Eventually, Major General turned toward me and said, "Rick, your classes influence a lot of companies and a lot of people. Here is something you ought to tell them. If those people respected their companies with one-tenth of one percent of the honor and respect that soldiers have for that flag, those people will always succeed."

Can you say something like that about your company?

One week later, the General sent me this incredible poem:

## My Name is Old Glory
*By Howard Schnauber*

I am the flag of the United States of America.
My name is Old Glory.

I fly atop the world's tallest buildings.
I stand watch in America's halls of justice.
I fly majestically over great institutes of learning.
I stand guard with the greatest military power in the world.

Look up! And see me!

I stand for peace, honor, truth, and justice.
I stand for freedom.
I am confident; I am arrogant.
I am proud.

When I am flown with my fellow banners,
My head is a little higher,
My colors a little truer.
I bow to no one.

I am recognized all over the world.
I am worshipped - I am saluted - I am respected
I am revered - I am loved, and I am feared.

I have fougt every battle of every war for more than 200 years:

Gettysburg, Shiloh, Appomattox, San Juan Hill, the trenches of France, the Argonne Forest, Anzio, Rome, the beaches of Normandy, the deserts of Africa, the cane fields of the Philippines, the rice paddies and jungles of Guam, Okinawa, Japan, Korea, Vietnam, Guadalcanal, New Britain, Peleliu, and many more islands. And a score of places long forgotten by all but those who were with me.

I was there.
I led my soldiers – I followed them.
I watched over them.
They loved me.

I was on a small hill in Iwo Jima.
I was dirty, battle-worn and tired, but my soldiers cheered me, and I was proud.

I have been soiled, burned, torn, and trampled on the streets of countries I have helped set free.

It does not hurt, for I am invincible.

I have been soiled, burned, torn, and trampled on the streets of my country, and when it is by those with whom I have served in battle - it hurts. But I shall overcome - for I am strong.

I have slipped the bonds of Earth and stand watch over the uncharted new frontiers of space from my vantage point on the moon.

I have been a silent witness to all of America's finest hours.

But my finest hour comes when I am torn into strips to be used for bandages for my wounded comrades on the field of battle,

When I fly at half mast to honor my soldiers,

And when I lie in the trembling arms of a grieving mother at the grave side of her fallen son.

I am proud.
My name is Old Glory.
Dear God – Long may I wave.

"Freedom is not free. Freedom has a price, and so does success. The next time you see a member of our military, thank them for serving their country and yours."

---

### Succeeding Inside the Box is Easy...
*We live in the greatest country in the world with every opportunity. Seize the opportunities.*

# YOUR COOKIES

*The Cookie Thief - by Valerie Cox*

A woman was waiting at an airport one night

With several long hours before her flight

She hunted for a book in the airport shop

Bought a bag of cookies and found a place to drop

She was engrossed in her book but happened to see

That the man beside her as bold as could be

Grabbed a cookie or two from the bag between

Which she tried to ignore to avoid a scene

She munched cookies and watched the clock

As this gutsy cookie thief diminished her stock

She was getting more irritated as the minutes ticked by

Thinking "If I wasn't so nice I'd blacken his eye"

With each cookie she took he took one too

And when only one was left she wondered what he'd do

With a smile on his face and a nervous laugh

He took the last cookie and broke it in half

He offered her half as he ate the other

She snatched it from him and thought "Oh brother

This guy has some nerve and he's also rude

Why he didn't even show any gratitude"

She had never known when she had been so galled

And sighed with relief when her flight was called

She gathered her belongings and headed for the gate

Refusing to look back at the thieving ingrate

She boarded the plane and sank in her seat

Then sought her book which was almost complete

As she reached in her baggage she gasped with surprise

There was her bag of cookies in front of her eyes

"If mine are here" she moaned with despair

"Then the others were his and he tried to share"

"Too late to apologize she realized with grief"

That she was the rude one, the ingrate, the thief.

---

### Succeeding Inside the Box is Easy...

*Never assume. We all know what assume stands for.*

*Do not judge too quickly. Things are not always what they seem.*

## YOUR HAPPINESS

The "Declaration of Independence" identifies the basic rights of life, liberty, and the pursuit of happiness.

At a very basic level, most people just want to be happy.

Many people claim they are motivated by money. In my experience, though, the only time money is a prime motivator is when you do not have any. It is always a wonderful indicator of integrity. If you do not have enough money, will you do unscrupulous things to get it?

If one of my employees told me that they were motivated by money exclusively, I would feel like I had to watch them all the time. Could I trust such a person?

If a person is motivated by nothing but money, it always makes me anxious, especially about my wallet.

I do not define happiness by money. I define happiness in a very unique way:

"If you want to be happy for an hour, take a nap.

If you want to be happy for day, go golfing, fishing, or shopping.

If you want to be happy for a month, get married.

If you want to be happy for a year, inherit a fortune.

If you want to be happy for a lifetime, serve other people."

All human beings want a sense of well-being and happiness, and they will work hard to achieve it.

---

### Succeeding Inside the Box is Easy...
*Always remember there is no higher calling than serving others.*

# YOUR DASH

Sooner or later, everyone will be lying underneath a tombstone. On that tombstone will be a dash. On one side of that dash will be the date of your birth; on the other side, the date of your death.

Do you know what that dash represents? All the time you spent on this earth. How will you spend your dash?

*Anonymous*

"I read of a man who stood up to speak at the funeral of a friend.

He referred to the dates on her tombstone from the beginning to the end.

He noted that first came her date of birth and spoke the following date with tears. He said what mattered most of all was the dash between those years.

For that dash represents all the time that she had spent alive on the earth.

And now only those who loved her know what that little line is worth.

For it matters not how much we own, the cars, the house, the cash.

What matters most is how we live and love and how we spend our dash.

So think about it long and hard, are there things you would like to change?

For you never know how much time is left that can still be rearranged.

If we could just slow down enough to consider what is true and real ,and try to understand the way other people feel.

Be less quick to anger and show appreciation more, and love the people in our lives like we've never loved them before.

Treat each other with respect and more often wear a smile, remembering this special dash might only last a while.

So when your eulogy is being read, with your life's actions to rehash, would you be proud of the things they say, about how you spent your dash?"

What kind of effect do you have on other people?

You will not be remembered for how tall you were; you will be remembered for how many times you bent down to teach others.

---

### Succeeding Inside the Box is Easy...
*Make others feel good, show appreciation and respect.*
*What will others say about the way you lived your dash?*

# BEHIND THE BUSINESS

## YOUR CALL TO ACTION

Pretend for a moment that you lived during the time period of Abraham Lincoln. Would a man like Honest Abe enjoy listening to someone like you? President Lincoln loved to listen to Dr. Gurley.

Often, to relieve a little stress, Lincoln would prop his door open and eavesdrop on the speeches Dr. Gurley was giving in the room next door.

On one occasion, an aide caught Lincoln eavesdropping.

Startled, the aide asked, "Mr. President, did you enjoy the speech?"

"Yes," Lincoln said. "I enjoyed it. It was well thought out. It was very enjoyable."

"Well, if you liked it that much," the aide said, "the impact of the speech will probably last a long time."

"Oh, no," Lincoln said. "This time, Dr. Gurley's speech had no impact on me at all."

Confused, the aide said, "Why?"

"Well," Lincoln said, "Dr. Gurley is a great speaker. However on this occasion, Dr. Gurley forgot to tell his audience to take action and to do something."

All the knowledge in the world is worthless without action.

Even if you fail, you will learn.

---

*Succeeding Inside the Box is Easy...*
*Start today and take action.*

## MAGIC PILLS

You do not need a magic pill. You do not need to hire new sales people, add inventory, or purchase expensive marketing. You do not need to think outside the box.

What you need is exceptional customer service. Your company must be so good that they cannot be ignored. The simpler you keep your strategy, the stronger your company will get.

Never assume that superficial company education or hand-out booklets are the answer. They will not last. Work on consistency and providing great customer service. If you have hired the right employees, great customer service is automatic and free.

A good friend of mine went into a drugstore and made a purchase. Printed on his receipt were the following words: "Hi, I am Rose, and I am here to serve you with our Seven Service Basics." Intrigued, he asked her, "What exactly are your Seven Service Basics?" Rose shrugged. "I do not know."

A few days later, he went back into the same store and bought another product. This time, his receipt read: "Hi, I am Octavia, and I am here to serve you with our Seven Service Basics." He looked at her. "Octavia, what exactly are your Seven Service Basics?" "I don't know," Octavia said.

Somewhere back at the corporate office, the Seven Service Basics made sense. The company created a manual, did some superficial training, and put some words on the customer's receipt. They thought they had found the magic pill. Stop selling your product and start solving your customers' problems.

---

### Succeeding Inside the Box is Easy...
*Do the little things, do them correctly and consistently.*

# INTERNAL COMBUSTION

Below are three rules that govern the marketplace:

**Rule # 1:**
A company can only be successful if it delights one internal customer and one external customer at a time. When customers enter your business, your service should make each of them feel like a king or a queen.

**Rule # 2:**
Rule #1 can only be achieved with happy, inspired employees.

**Rule # 3:**
Employees will never treat anyone any better than they are being treated themselves.

How is the morale in your company? Bad morale is like a painfully slow death. If morale is bad in your company, then I can guarantee you that your customer service is even worse. You need to out-service the competition, not out-smart them.

---

### *Succeeding Inside the Box is Easy...*
*Take good care of your internal customers. Then, trust them to take good care of your external customers.*

## MELT THE CHEESE

McDonald's has more than 30,000 locations, and they have been serving hamburgers for more than forty-seven years.

Recently, I read in the Wall Street Journal that McDonald's spent $680 million dollars on marketing and new franchises, and they lost money. Why? They lost focus of what brought them to the mountain. They began to concentrate on franchising, not on their customers. They were a great example of a company that got back on track

Out of the ten goals they set for themselves, three struck me as vitally important:

1) Serve the food hot

2) Keep the restaurants clean and updated

3) Melt the cheese

You may laugh at such simple goals. McDonald's got back to the basics and they succeeded. The last time I checked, McDonald's stock was up. Why? Because they realized the little things make a big difference.

Please note that, all along, McDonald's was consistent. Consistency is an important component of success, as I have already mentioned. McDonald's actually took being consistent too far. They replaced the words on the register keys with pictures. They resolved to make the process so easy, that a pimply faced high school kid could run the entire store. And that's exactly where they went wrong. They forgot about service. They forgot to serve their food hot, to keep their restaurants clean and updated, and to melt the cheese on their burgers. They forgot to be consistent at customer service.

---

*Succeeding Inside the Box is Easy...*
*Those who service the best profit the most.*

# GOOD CHOICE

Want your company to stand out in a crowd? Ask your internal and external customers what can you do to improve your business?

According to a study by U.S. News and World Report, seventy-four percent of customers stop using a business because of an employee's indifferent attitude.

Have you ever had a memorable reaction to someone who took your order at a drive-through window?

A few years ago, I approached the drive-through window at a Chick-fil-A restaurant. If you are like me, most of the time, I can barely understand what the person inside is saying. However, on this particular occasion, I was pleasantly surprised.

"Welcome to Chick-fil-A," a voice said. "Would you like to try a combo?"

First of all, I could understand what he was saying.

Second, he used proper English. "Yes," I said. "I would like to try a chicken combo." "Good choice," he said with enthusiasm.

This particular employee complimented me on my good choice. I could not wait to eat that sandwich.

How many people do you compliment? How long can you maintain a passion about what you do?

"Passion persuades, and that fuels belief." Never underestimate the power of purpose and more importantly passion.

---

*Succeeding Inside the Box is Easy...*
*Be passionate about what you do. People are persuaded more by the depth of you conviction than the height of your logic, more by your enthusiasm than any proof you have to offer.*

# THE PRODUCT IS NOT IMPORTANT

All products look alike, no matter whether you sell jets or Jello. That is why you should not try to exceed your customers' expectations. Instead, concentrate first on being consistent with your level of customer service.

For over eighteen years, I have traveled 250 days a year. One of my routes started in Yuma, Arizona, then on to Los Angles, California. My favorite was the red-eye flight from Los Angles to Dulles, Virginia, then on to Philadelphia. Sometimes, layovers kept me in an airport for eight hours straight. I would be tired, jet-lagged and dirty. Other times, I would be in the air for hours, sleeping with 250 of my closest, grimy friends.

After the plane touched down, we would all be dirty and exhausted. Stepping off that plane, all I wanted to do was get to my rental car, head for the hotel, take a shower, and prepare for my next speech.

On one horrid occasion, a rental car company van pulled up to the curb. The driver scowled at me. Everything about his body language yelled, "Get in the van." He never actually said a word. Sometimes, a person's body language is far more important than their words. Have you ever interacted with a person whose mouth is saying one thing, while their body language is saying something else? This particular driver was text-book rude. He definitely did not want me in that van. On this occasion, I was even more tired and dirty than usual. Quite frankly, this particular driver looked like Satan's first cousin. "Are you a regular or preferred customer?" he snapped. "I am preferred," I said, stepping inside the van.

As soon as I sat down, guess what was going through my mind? I was wondering if the rental van was safe. I was arguing with myself about whether I had paid too much for this ride. I was making a note to research another van service.

Here is the important factor.

All of this occurred within thirty seconds of meeting that driver. First impressions are important. That driver did not think he was in sales. He believed he was just the driver of a company van. He did not realize the impact he was making on customers. Otherwise, why would I have been suddenly so concerned with my safety and how expensive my rental car was going to be? One rude driver is all it took. And I guarantee you the driver never even realized he was having that kind of effect. Regardless, I never used that rent-a-car company again. Next time, I decided to go with a different rent-a-car company. Just like before, after taking the red-eye flight, I got off the airplane. As always just like before, a van pulls up to the curb.

However, this time, the driver opens the door and says, "Welcome to Philadelphia!" Then, he put the van in park and ran toward me. At first, I thought he was going to fight me. But guess why he was running? He was running to pick up my luggage. Suddenly, I am smiling. I like this situation. This driver knows all rent-a-car companies look alike. Yet, he is making me feel good about me.

Mr. Grandinetti are you preferred or regular?" this new driver asked. "I am preferred," I said. "Great! My name's Hugh."

By now, I have got a happy bounce in my step. What I am not thinking about is the safety of the car, or the price of the rent-a-car. Within thirty to forty-five seconds of meeting one individual from this new company I am hoping my ride in the van lasts a little longer than usual.

When I got off the van, the driver handed me my luggage and said, "Mr. Grandinetti, you have a good day." "Now, I will." I said.

I was so blown away by Hugh's customer service that I wrote a letter to his company. At a ceremony in front of his peers, Hugh received $75.00 and a gift certificate. All Hugh did was his job. Hugh did not have to think outside the box. What he did was not new-fangled, or outrageous.

Hugh succeeded inside the box.

---

### Succeeding Inside the Box is Easy...
*Service is so poor in the United States that if someone just does their job and does it consistently he or she will dominate the market.*

# THE WINNER'S CIRCLE

## ARE YOU A WINNER

When I think of winners, I think of a good friend of mine.

He was from Cuba. Originally, he descended from a wealthy family. In the late 1950s, however, Fidel Castro came to power, and his father lost his company, and all his family's money to the new regime. He went from wealth to poverty over night.

A generation later, his family was living in the United States. Here in the United States they have prospered. They live in a prestigious neighborhood. Once, in a quiet conversation, he told me, "My kids do not like it when I say this, because I live in a very nice part of town. I live in this prestigious neighborhood because of one thing: I clean toilets for a living". You see, winners do things that losers do not want to do. "I am proud that I clean toilets." Even today, he is a successful businessman in more ways than one.

Sometimes, we Americans get lazy and complacent and comfortable. Do not let that be your story.

---

*Succeeding Inside the Box is Easy...*
*Be consistent in what you do. Be a person of action. Be a winner like my friend.*

# PAY IT FORWARD

Ever notice the general demeanor of people in an airport?

Not many people are smiling. Maybe they are lonely. Maybe they have jet-lag. Maybe they are just preoccupied.

Once, I was in an international airport deli, having a sandwich. After I finished, I walked across the deli to throw away my trash. My hands were full. The lid of the garbage can was filthy, and it was one of those garbage cans with a lid you had to flip open. Nearby there was a lady and her daughter. The lady and the little girl opened the lid for me. "Thank you so much," I said. I could not help but notice that she had gotten her hands filthy in the process, just to help me.

Never underestimate the potential of a simple act of courtesy. It is an action of paying it forward.

A few minutes later, I noticed an elderly woman walking toward the same garbage can. Her hands were just as full as mine had been. The lid was just as nasty for her as it had been before. I pushed back the garbage can lid for her almost without thinking and my hands got dirty, too. Something bothered me a little. Was I that nice by nature? No. It was because someone had modeled the behavior for me.

The little girl reminded me by her actions how meaningful it is to help other people.

There is no opportunity too small to pay it forward when someone helps you.

---

### Succeeding Inside the Box is Easy...
*Can you think of something you could do in the business world that might make all the difference in somebody's day? The smaller the better. The nastier the garbage can lid, the stronger the impact.*

## YOU CAN ALWAYS LEARN

Let me tell you about a friend of mine named Dale. He is with the Cocopah Indian Tribe, out of Yuma, Arizona. A few years ago, Dale and I discovered that his tribe needed a writing course, so we attended one together, just to get some ideas.

The teacher was not the best educator. She was so horrible, in fact, that after forty-five minutes, I completely shut her out, and used the rest of my time in the classroom to start writing a letter of apology to Dale, because I felt like I wasted his time.

When the class was over, Dale said, "What did you think of the course?" I had the presence of mind to answer with a question. "What did you think?"

"It was not the best," Dale answered, "however, I did learn four things." Then, he looked at me and said, "I will take action on those four things."

To this day, every time Dale corresponds with me, he puts a little yellow sticky note on the correspondence, reminding me of the four things he learned that day. It is an excellent reminder, because even though Dale only graduated from high school, he is a much smarter man than I am. Why? Because that day, he chose to learn, and I did not.

"Rick, I do not have all those fancy degrees that you do," he often reminds me, "so I have to learn every chance I get. Quite frankly, when I come across a problem, I apply common sense to it, and usually it works."

What a shame I chose not to learn that day, because I did not like the instructor. Dale told me "readers are leaders."

---

*Succeeding Inside the Box is Easy...*
*Never stop learning.*

# JOHN, THE TOILET BOWL SALESPERSON

Years ago, I was planning a move to northern Virginia, and we considered buying a house on the side of a mountain.

The builder told me I needed a septic tank. I had heard a lot of bad things about septic tanks, horror stories about problems with back-ups and sewage leaks. The builder understood my apprehension, and offered a suggestion.

"You need to talk to our toilet bowl salesperson. His name is John." I am not kidding. His real name was John.

When I entered the showroom, I was greeted by a gentleman in a suit. His name tag read 'Toilet Bowl Salesperson John.'

"You must be Mr. Grandinetti," John said. "The builder told me about your issues, and I certainly understand your dilemma, as well as your fear. Do not worry. I will help you every step of the way with your septic tank needs."

John turned out to be more than passionate about septic tanks. Can you imagine? More importantly, John was deeply concerned about helping me solve my problem. "You know," John said, "what you need is called 'the Turbo Flush.'"

"What?" I asked. "The Turbo Flush," he explained, "is so powerful that it can flush a cat down the toilet." John was passionate about toilets.

What are you passionate about? Do you get excited about anything? Do you have a job or a career?

---

***Succeeding Inside the Box is Easy...***
*Love what you do.*

# YOU NEED A BIGGER PROBLEM

Want a sure-fire way to realize how good you really have it? Hold your problem up against a really big problem.

Long ago, I was sitting in an airport terminal, waiting for my flight. I think it is important that you know this happens to everyone; even me, you see I was a little down on myself.

Do you believe things happen for a reason? I sure do.

Suddenly, across the terminal, I heard a big ruckus. I looked up to see a mob of people getting off a plane.

My bad mood was still controlling the internal conversation I was having with myself. I was interested enough in the ruckus to figure out exactly what was going on.

It turned out to be a group of teenagers with an average age of maybe fifteen, or so. Something was weirdly unusual they were all tied together, literally.  They were all laughing and having fun, and they were literally tied together with rope.

I looked a little closer. Suddenly I realized they were all blind. It was not the rope that held them all together.

It was pure faith in the person just ahead of them in the chain. This reliance on others, whom they knew and loved, made their blindness almost irrelevant.

How do I know that? Because they were laughing and having fun.

I reconsidered my bad mood I was having. You see, I was healthy. I had 20/20 vision, and I only thought I had a problem. What I really needed was a bigger problem.

---

*Succeeding Inside the Box is Easy...*
*Be thankful for what you have.*

# KEEP SHINING

Todd called himself 'the shoeshine boy.'

He was a friend of mine and one that I will never forget.

At one point in my career, I traveled through the Philadelphia airport once a week. This was where I first met Todd.

The next step in this story is not fun for me to share. Why? Because I am embarrassed to say that, at that point in my life, I was a little bit of a jerk. Hard to believe, I know. Life had a very significant lesson for me to learn in that airport.

Also, you should know that I am extremely meticulous about my shoes. That is an understatement. Therefore, Todd and I were meant to meet.

The story starts when I first realized that Todd was stalking me. We had never met before; Todd made no bones about following me around. He stared at me; stalked me really.

About the time I had decided to run toward airport security, Todd crept up to me with a strange gleam in his eye and said, "Let me shine your shoes."

I pointed toward the floor in hot anger. "Can't you tell I shine these all the time? Go bother somebody else!"

Todd's shoulders slumped down, and he slowly backed away. After he had achieved a safe distance from me, he looked up humbly and said, "I'll do a good job. Let me shine your shoes."

Even though I had just given him a full blast of my arrogance, Todd remained humble. I realized, if I ever wanted to feel good about myself again, I needed to self-correct the situation with Todd.

"Come on over," I said, hoping my smile would suffice as an apology.

Then, Todd knelt down next to me. He gently lifted my shoe up onto his portable shoeshine box like it was a six-hundred dollar piece of leather. He prepared his polish and towel like they were expensive tools. Soon, Todd was 'in the zone.' As he got caught up in his intensity of shining my shoes and his attention to detail and focusing on his craft, I forgot about my own problems.

With a refined expertise, at this exact moment, Todd asked me a question. "Was your day successful?"

"Yeah," I lied. "It was." "Well," he paused, "what did you do?"

I was shocked. Looking up from my feet was a shoeshine boy who was talking to me like he was my equal.

I continued watching Todd, and talking to him, until his speed slowed a little.

Snap! Todd had popped his towel in a startling way to let me know he had finished. I almost felt like giving him a round of applause. Now, Todd stood up. "Mr. Grandinetti, are the shoes to your satisfaction?"

"Yes, Todd," I said. "What do I owe you?"

He looked me straight in the eye and said, "Whatever you think they are worth."

This was my first interaction with Todd, so I did not know it at that time, however I do now. Todd was the highest paid shoeshine boy in the state.

Not only was it what he did, the key was how he did it.

That one shoeshine changed everything. From that time forward, whenever I was in Philadelphia, I stalked Todd. I usually found him. I certainly enjoyed being around him. The truth was, I was not stalking him to get my shoes shined, although I am very fastidious about my shoes. I wanted the feeling that Todd gave me.

If it makes any difference, Todd was mentally challenged.

However, you can learn a lot from Todd. I know I sure did.

### *Succeeding Inside the Box is Easy...*

*Todd's story exemplifies everything you need to succeed. Be consistent in what you do and have passion about what you do. Give an extra 1% everyday, treat others the way you want to be treated, live your life passionately; it is a gift and many have made the ultimate sacrifice so that you can live in our great nation. And finally and most importantly, serve others. You never know when you will influence someone else in your acts personally or professionally.*

## Note from Rick Grandinetti

I hope you have enjoyed reading this book.

The stories and examples presented in this book exemplify the things I believe, and the lessons I have learned, over my entire career.

Please read these stories whenever you need encouragement or a reminder.

Spend more time looking for "Success Inside the Box".

*–Rick Grandinetti*

---

Succeed Inside The Box
PO Box 5684
Cary, North Carolina 27512

www.succeedinsidethebox.com

56597327R00035

Made in the USA
Lexington, KY
26 October 2016